BORNEO

A PHOTOGRAPHIC JOURNEY

Dennis Lau

TRAVELCOM ASIA

BORNEO - A PHOTOGRAPHIC JOURNEY

Published by
Travelcom Asia Sdn Bhd (Company No. 302900-K)
117-B, 3rd Floor, Lot 132 Ban Hock Road
93100 Kuching, Sarawak, Malaysia

E-mail: tlcs@pc.jaring.my

First published 1999.

Photographs by   : Dennis Lau
Text by   : Wayne Tarman & Mike Reed
Design & Layout by : C&D Design Advertising Sdn Bhd (218813-M)
Printed in Malaysia

ISBN 983-99431-1-1

CONTENTS

INTRODUCTION

Sarawak & Sabah

Sarawak and Sabah - the two states that make up the Malaysian part of Borneo - are neighbours, but they have many striking differences; in geography, in history, and in the ethnic mix that makes up their vibrant cultures. Together, they offer the keen-eyed observer a striking insight into life on the world's third largest island.

Sarawak, the larger of the two states, is a land of rivers and rainforests, of thousands of longhouse communities hidden deep in the jungle, left very much to their own devices under the White Rajahs, and only brought into the economic and social mainstream after World War II. Sabah also has rivers and rainforests, but its geography is altogether more dramatic, thanks to the mighty Mount Kinabalu, and it is much more a maritime society, with a large proportion of the population living near (and even on) the sea.

Both of these states are populated by peoples with rich and colourful cultures, and have attracted explorers, writers and artists since time immemorial. Painters and engravers found abundant sources of inspiration, and many of the 19th century drawings, painting and sketches that have survived are quite exquisite. But none of them portrayed the warmth and spontaneity of life in Borneo. To capture Borneo it is necessary to capture the moment, and this had to wait for the arrival of the photographers.

European Photographers - The Early Pioneers

Although Borneo offers an endless supply of fascinating visual images, early photographers were discouraged by the problems of transporting heavy equipment through difficult terrain, and protecting their delicate lenses and glass plates from the tropical humidity. It was not until the late 1880's that any serious attempt was made to document Borneo in photographs.

In Sarawak, European officers of the Brooke administration played a pioneering role in the photographic documentation of people and traditions. The most famous of these was Charles Hose, who joined the Sarawak Civil Service in 1884. Hose was a keen ethnographer, and one of the pioneers of visual anthropology. His photographs of Sarawak in the late 19th Century provide an important visual record of the period, and some superb examples are found in his books, *The Pagan Tribes of Borneo* (Cass, London, 1966 [1912]) and *Natural Man* (Oxford University Press, Singapore, 1988 [1926]).

In neighbouring Kalimantan, the Dutch philanthropist and social commentator H.F. Tillema spent over a decade photographing and filming the people of the interior. His *A Journey Among the Peoples of Borneo in Words & Pictures* (OUP, Oxford, 1989 [1938]) provides a graphic account of rural life during the early 20th Century.

Except for the occasional news picture, little more came out of Borneo in the following decades, thanks to the Great Depression and World War II. It was not until the 1950's that Tom Harrisson, the curator of the Sarawak Museum, began photographing the people as he went about his ethnographic research. During the same period, Hedda Morrison, highly acclaimed for her pictures of pre-war China, spent 15 years photographing the people of Sarawak. Morrison was an acute social observer with a keen photographic eye, and her work captured the rhythm of daily life in the longhouses. Some of her best photographs appear in *Life in a Longhouse* (Borneo Literature Bureau, Kuching, 1962) and *Sarawak* (MacGibbon & Kee, London, 1957), both exceptional records of everyday life in a rapidly changing society.

It is worth noting that during colonial times, Sabah was less well photographed than Sarawak. This is perhaps due to the ways in which the two states were governed. Sabah was a commercial colony run by the British North Borneo Company, who discouraged "unnecessary" visitors, whilst the colourful Brooke Regime in Sarawak attracted a steady stream of adventurers, naturalists, and anthropologists.

Pioneering Local Photographers

The post-war period at last saw the emergence of local photographers. Previously, those few locals who owned cameras used them to earn a living, producing portraits and wedding photos. However, local photographers began to make an impact from the mid 1950's onwards. In Sabah, photographic societies were active in Sandakan and Tawau, whilst in Sarawak individual photographers based in Kuching and Sibu started to make frequent trips upriver to document the peoples and cultures of the interior. Both Sarawakian and Sabahan photographers also started to submit their work to international salons and the work of local photographers started to appear in print.

The most important local photographer during this time was K.F. Wong, a master portraitist and the first Sarawakian photographer to submit his work to international salons. The owner of a studio in Kuching, Wong had trained in Xiamen, China, and had a technical mastery of his equipment that few modern photographers could match. Although he ran a studio to generate income, K.F. Wong treated photography as an art. Whenever he could escape from his busy studio, he would head for the interior, where he produced exquisite portraits of the tribal people, and documented important historical events.

Throughout the 1950's he compiled a superb collection of beautifully lit portraits and striking candid shots, many of which were included in his first book *Pagan Innocence* (Jonathan Cape, London, 1960). Although the title and introductory text reflected the colonial attitudes of the time, K.F. Wong's photographs spoke for themselves, and established him as the father of Borneo photography.

During his long career K.F. Wong contributed to a number of publications, from locally published school books to academic publications, magazines and art books. His last book, *Borneo Scenes* (Anna Photo Company,

Kuching, 1979), was a collection of both black & white and colour photos of Sabah, Sarawak and Brunei. In addition to the superb black and white tribal images that K.F. Wong was famous for, the book included some exquisite colour images of the people of Borneo, as well as photos of historic events.

Whilst K.F. Wong extolled the beauty of Sarawak's people, Lim Poh Chiang documented upriver communities and the chance encounters he experienced. Lim grew up with the Ibans in the riverside village of Song, and spoke their language fluently. A self-taught photographer, he made frequent trips into the interior throughout the 1950's and 1960's in order to source antiques and handicrafts for his antique shop in Sibu. During these antique-buying trips Lim usually carried his camera so that he could photograph the various ethnic groups he met on his upriver travels. Some of his most famous photos were taken in 1962 when he met a group of Penan from Indonesia who had crossed the border and set up camp in Sarawak. These are included in *Among The Dayaks* (Graham Brash, Singapore, 1989), a fascinating collection of both posed and candid shots, and a ruggedly naturalistic record of a society that was, in Lim's own words, "Poised at that fragile, tranquil prelude on the threshold of change."

K.F. Wong and Lim Poh Chiang were not the only photographers working in Sarawak at the time. The Sarawak Museum also employed a number of local photographers and their work provided the museum with an extensive ethnographic record. Unfortunately, however, far less similar work was done in Sabah. The reason for this remains a matter for conjecture, but it is possible that Sabah-based photographers, lacking a tradition of ethnographic photography, preferred to devote their efforts to the state's remarkable landscapes and more conventional portrait shots.

Bearer of a Great Tradition

Surprisingly, the pioneering work of K.F. Wong did not give rise to a generation of eager young photographers keen to carry on documenting longhouse life. Although there are many talented photographers in Sarawak and Sabah, very few have devoted their skills to documenting peoples and cultures, upriver life and social change.

Throughout the 1980's a number of Sarawakian photographers focused on capturing *kampung* life, whilst in Sabah shooting faces of the people at Sabah's *tamu* (native markets) was popular. Although the subject matter of this *kampung* and *tamu* work was the people of Borneo, it was basically urban-based photography. From the 1990's onwards, local photographers have focused more on Borneo's environment than its people. The attractions of Sarawak and Sabah's national parks - a rich source of subject material for the nature photographer - have attracted many of the environmentally aware younger generation, who are focusing their efforts on nature and wildlife, and producing some excellent work.

The special challenges of ethnographic photography are another reason for the relative scarcity of photographers in this field. To capture the essence of Borneo's indigenous people and their culture requires patience, stamina and insight, with little prospect of financial reward. Very few photographers have these qualities, or the time and inclination to apply them. One who does, though, is Dennis Lau.

For the last 40 years Dennis, a Sarawakian of mixed Chinese-Melanau descent, has worked as a photo-journalist and ethnographic photographer in virtually every corner of Sarawak, Sabah and Brunei. He is undoubtedly one of Malaysia's best photo-journalists, widely respected for his unique images of tribal peoples, the fruits of extended field trips into the interior or '*ulu*' regions of Borneo.

Although Dennis has travelled throughout Borneo he has naturally placed greater emphasis on his home state of Sarawak. Through the lens of his camera he has documented the changes and upheavals facing Sarawak's native peoples in a time of rapid social change, recording colourful customs and traditions, living cultures, vanishing lifestyles and moments from the past. Whether the subject matter is a tattooed Iban elder, a Bidayuh shaman, or a Penan family trekking to a new hunting ground, his photographs clearly demonstrate the deep respect and high regard that he feels for Borneo's indigenous people. Yet they are not merely ethnographic records: many of his black and white studies are classic examples of the portraitist's art.

The way a photographer interacts with his or her subject is often reflected in the photos. Dennis' personality certainly helps in this respect. He is unassuming, friendly and softly spoken, and has the knack of making people relax and get on with their life as if the camera is not there.

Dennis Lau has that rare ability to look at his subject objectively and gain what could be considered an out-sider's view, whilst using his local knowledge and language skills to gain the kind of access that only insiders are allowed. This remarkable combination - the detachment of the outsider and the access of the insider - enables Dennis to achieve both the honesty and the intimacy that all great photographers strive for.

Bintulu was a sleepy backwater when Dennis was growing up there, not the oil and gas boom-town it is today. A neighbour ran a small photo studio and Dennis soon become a darkroom assistant. At first he carried buckets of water and peered over his neighbour's shoulder to watch the images appear in the developing trays. It wasn't long before Dennis was allowed to expose and develop film. He borrowed a camera and started to take photos for the first time, focusing on landscapes rather than people.

At the age of 19 Dennis won second prize in the Borneo Photographic Competition and through this he met his hero, the remarkable K.F. Wong. Wong encouraged Dennis and gave him hints on the technical side of photography. These kind words from a master photographer were all the inspiration he needed.

In 1960 Dennis joined the teaching profession and was sent to a small rural school located north of Bintulu. This up-country location essentially shaped the development of Dennis' photography. The school was isolated and so Dennis started to travel extensively at weekends, sometimes going home to Bintulu but more often than not visiting the longhouses of some of his pupils. He always carried a camera, and so began a photographic journey that has lasted for over 40 years and brought him into contact with almost all of Sarawak's tribal groups, as well as the major ethnic groups in Sabah.

Dennis entered the Sarawak Teacher's Training College in Sibu in 1963, where he met and later married Chiew Pik Hung. A patient and understanding person, she quickly got used to Dennis disappearing into the interior on extended trips. Following completion of the course Dennis was posted to Miri, which gave him further opportunities to head into the interior and photograph Sarawak's people. He also caught the attention of the Bishop of Miri, A. D. Galvin, who gave early encouragement and helped financially with film expenses and trips up the Baram River. About this time Dennis started reading *Life* magazine, and

The late Bishop of Miri, the Right Reverend A.D. Galvin, celebrates midnight mass in a Kenyah longhouse. Tinjar River, Christmas 1974.

became aware of the important role of the photo-journalist. He was inspired by the *Life* photographers' photo essays, and decided to devote himself to photo-journalism.

In 1976 Dennis was asked to contribute photos to the Brunei-based Borneo Bulletin. The small retainer from his weekly photo column "*Dennis Lau's Borneo*" (which is still going strong today) allowed him to spend more money on film, and to travel further afield. It was during this period that Dennis discovered the visual charms of Sabah and Brunei, and made the occasional journey to Indonesian Kalimantan. But it was a chance encounter in Sarawak that led to international recognition and critical acclaim.

On Christmas Eve in 1968 Dennis was staying at Long San, a Kenyah longhouse on the Upper Baram River, when a small group of Penan wandered into the village to seek medical attention at a missionary clinic. This marked the beginning of Dennis' long association with these masters of the rainforest. Over the next 20 years he made a number of trips into the interior to meet up with the Penan, staying with them for weeks at a time and taking part in their tough, nomadic way of life. The longer he spent with them, the more his respect for the Penan grew.

Almost twenty years after their first encounter, Dennis published *Penans - The Vanishing Nomads of Borneo* (Inter-State Publishing, Kota Kinabalu, 1987), a black and white photo essay and personal record of his time with these remarkable people. The book offers an insight into the fast-disappearing lifestyle of a tribe that has been heavily featured in the international media thanks to the Bruno Manser saga. Dennis Lau's black and white photos of the Penan are not voyeuristic, exploitative shots of tribal communities, they are images of real people, taken by a fellow Sarawakian who knows the word "respect".

Penans - The Vanishing Nomads of Borneo was widely acclaimed, and following its publication Dennis was asked to contribute to a number of glossy coffee table books focusing on Malaysia and Borneo, including *This is Borneo, Crafts of Malaysia* and *Malaysia - Heart of South-East Asia*. His work was featured in major publications, including *The Far Eastern Economic Review, Asiaweek, Stern, Mission Aktuell* and *GEO Special*. Dennis' photographs have also been exhibited at international salons in Australia, Britain, Brunei, India, Indonesia, Japan, Malaysia and Singapore. Yet first and foremost, Dennis still viewed photography as a hobby; it wasn't until he retired from teaching in 1993 that he started to receive paid photo assignments.

Recognition has come late for Dennis Lau, but it is all the sweeter for the long wait; his reputation in Sarawak is formidable, and his name is spoken in reverential tones. In 1998 formal recognition came from the Royal Photographic Society (UK), who made him their Overseas Service Representative for Malaysia - tacit admission that they see him as one Malaysia's best photographers. The relationship between Dennis and his homeland remains a mutually beneficial one - in

A Kayan craftswoman attends to her beadwork. Some superb examples of her work are on the wall behind her. Ulu Belaga, 1977.

recent years his images have been used for promoting Sarawak as a tourism destination. His only regret is that there are no youngsters pursuing his kind of photo-journalism. Dennis may have retired from teaching, but he certainly hasn't stopped taking photos. He still roams around Borneo doing what he does best - taking pictures of this vast island and its people.

Borneo - A Photographic Journey

Borneo - A Photographic Journey focuses on Dennis Lau's photographs of the people of Sarawak and Sabah, in northern Borneo. The photographs span the period from 1952 to 1999. The book is divided into sections featuring different ethnic groups. Each section is accompanied by brief introductory text and photo captions.

This book is meant to provide a glimpse of life in Borneo, not an ethnographic record. Fifteen ethnic groups from Sarawak and Sabah are featured, including major groups such as the Iban of Sarawak and Kadazan/Dusun of Sabah and smaller groups such as the Penan, Kelabit and Rungus. The book does not feature Indonesian Kalimantan. Nevertheless it represents over 40 years of dedicated work. To cover Kalimantan as well would take another 40 years.

This photographic essay adds to those by pioneering photographers who focused on capturing the peoples and cultures of Borneo. K.F. Wong and Lim Poh Chiang worked during a visually interesting period and were certainly able to capture images that are no longer around today. For Many people K.F. Wong's and Lim Poh Chiang's photographs represents the "real" Borneo, the tribal images that became the *leitmotif* of this vast island.

Dennis Lau's work covers a different period, a period of rapid change when "development" reached even the most geographically isolated community, a time when traditional dress started to give way to the ubiquitous T-Shirt. But cultures and traditions live on, adapting and evolving. Dennis has captured much of this change, and much that has remained the same.

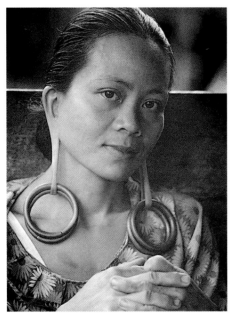

Portrait of a Sebop woman wearing large brass earrings. Long Luyang, Tinjar River, 1974.

For example, the *Gawai Antu* festival is as important as it ever was for the Iban; the bards may wear three-piece suits with their hornbill feather hats (see page 26) but they recite the same oral history as their forefathers. The Kenyah brewer may opt to store her rice wine in a Gordon's Gin Bottle instead of a ceramic jar (page 51) but the taste is a fiery as ever.

Like the early photographers, Dennis Lau's work forms an historic record. But his record is not about the way things were; it is about the way things change - about how the people of Sarawak and Sabah face the changes and the challenges of the late 20th century, with dignity, determination, and, as the photographs collected here so clearly show, with a sparkling sense of humour.

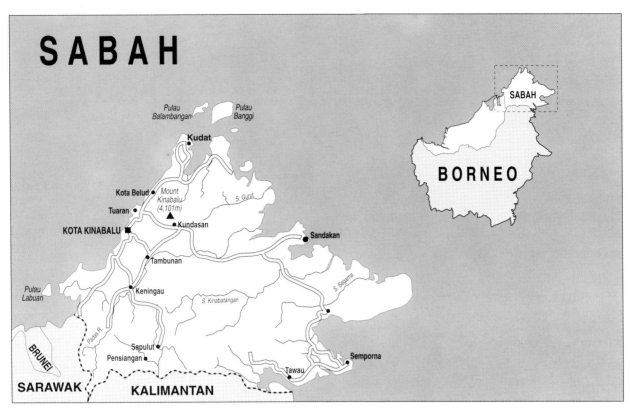

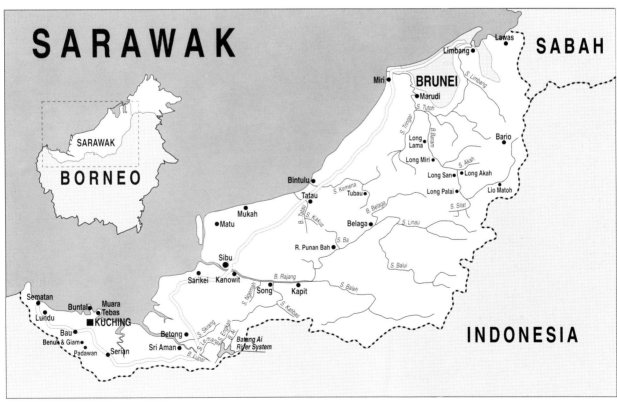

S = Sungai (River)   B = Batang (Major River)

The above maps highlight the places and rivers mentioned in this book.

SARAWAK
Bidayuh

The Bidayuh are the fourth-largest ethnic group in Sarawak, forming approximately 8% of the population. They are hill-rice farmers, dwelling in longhouses or villages at the foothills of Southwest Sarawak's rugged mountains. Formerly known as Land Dayaks (in contrast to the Iban Sea Dayaks), they are divided into five distinct dialect groups. The Bidayuh are masters at working with bamboo, which features in many of their arts and crafts and in the construction of their longhouses.

Left: A Bidayuh woman husks rice with a wooden rice mortar. The split bamboo floor of the longhouse can be clearly seen. Kampung Benuk, 1977.

Opposite: Bidayuh mother breast-feeding her child to sleep. Padawan. 1977.

The photos on this page were taken during *Gawai Padi*, an annual ritual usually held in June to give thanks to the rice spirit *(Semangat Padi)* for a good harvest.

Above: Priestesses divide the *arang* (offerings) between them and invite the rice spirit to enter their bodies. Kampung Benuk, 1977.

Right: *Semangat padi* has answered her summons as a priestess slowly recovers from her trance. A Shaman reassures her that all is well. Kampung Benuk, 1977.

Opposite: A Bidayuh lady takes a well earned rest after walking from her village near the Indonesian border to Anna Rais longhouse. Padawan, 1988.

Opposite: A Bidayuh priest (shaman) wearing a traditional circular rattan necklace decorated with glass beads, cowrie shells and bear claws. Kampung Benuk, 1977.

Below: Morning river scene at Kampung Giam, 1989.

SARAWAK
Chinese

The Chinese are the second largest ethnic group in Sarawak, comprising approximately 28% of the population. They are mostly descendants of migrants from Southern China who arrived between the 18th and early 20th centuries. They are a very diverse community; the eight major dialect groups (Hakka, Hokkien, Cantonese, Foochow, Chao Ann, Teochew, Henghua, Hainanese) include adherents of many different religions, including Taoism, Buddhism, Confucianism and Christianity. Their vibrant cultural life is one of the most colourful aspects of life in East Malaysia's towns and cities.

A Chinese pipe band, part of a temple procession, passes through the streets of Kuching, 1988.

An elderly Chinese lady at the Tua Pek Kong temple during Chinese New Year. Kuching 1985.

Above: A lion dance is performed at Muara Tebas Temple during Chinese New Year. The two 'clowns' to the left of the lion are comic characters that taunt and tease the lion, adding an element of fun, as he goes about the serious business of chasing away evil spirits. The lion dance is one of the most popular cultural components of Chinese New Year celebrations throughout the world. Muara Tebas, 1987.

Right: A group of children depicting characters from the "Journey to the West", a Chinese folk novel. In this well-known classic a monk embarks on a journey accompanied by three disciples: *Sun Wu Kung* - the Monkey King, *Chu Pa Chieh* - a pig spirit, and *Sha Monk* - a water demon. Along the way they meet demons and dragons and encounter all sorts of magic. The Journey to the West is loosely based on the true story of *Xuan Zang*, a famous monk who travelled to India to collect Buddhist scriptures and bring them back to China for translation. Kuching, 1988.

17

Above: A Chinese man with his face painted to depict the Monkey King, the mischievous hero of the folk novel "Journey to the West". This legendary quest is full of action and adventure and incorporates Chinese fables, myths, legends, superstitions and elements of Taoism and Buddhism. This photo was taken during celebrations to mark *Chap Goh Meh*, the last day of the Chinese New Year celebration. Bau, 1994.

Left: A master goldsmith in his workshop. Kuching, 1979

SARAWAK
Iban

The Iban are Sarawak's largest and best-known ethnic group. Aggressive and expansionist in the past, they were widely feared for their headhunting exploits. The Iban were also known as Sea Dayaks, due to their expertise with boats and their occasional involvement in piracy. They are fiercely egalitarian, and practise a simple form of democracy based around their own longhouse community. Traditionally they were shifting cultivators of hill rice, but nowadays more and more Iban farmers are moving into cash crops such as pepper, organising their land into plantations to grow rubber or oil palm, or moving to urban areas.

Left: Of all the ethnic groups of Borneo, the Iban are considered to be the most skilled weavers. Using backstrap looms they produce a range of textiles, the most important being the *pua kumbu*, a hand woven warp *ikat*. Traditionally, textile designs are infused with the notion of war (or head hunting) and the cultivation of *padi*. In traditional Iban culture, *padi* represents the source of life itself, whilst heads represent fertility. Lemanak River, 1989.

Opposite: An Iban maiden performs a welcome dance wearing a traditional costume complete with a range of silver adornments. Her sarong-type skirt is decorated with silver coins whilst she wears numerous silver bracelets, armlets and anklets and a magnificent *sugu tinggi*, a decorative silver head-dress. Iban silverware was traditionally made by Maloh silversmiths from West Kalimantan, who used to travel around Borneo, producing items of silverware to order. Kemena River, 1972.

Below: Exterior of a traditional Iban longhouse. The open verandah is known as the *tanju*. To the left of the staircase is the *ruai* (covered verandah) whilst the *bilik* (individual apartments) are situated to the right. The roof is made entirely of *belian* (ironwood) shingles. Labang River, Ulu Kemena, 1973.

Above: A traditional Iban healing ceremony. The *manang* (medicine man) summons the spirits to help him cure the sick child. The *pua kumbu* textiles worn by the *manang* and scattered on the floor are believed to have the power to ward off bad spirits. Ulu Tatau, 1973.

Left: A legacy of head-hunting. Skulls like these still play an important part in many Iban rituals. Nanga Serubah, Lemanak River, 1999.

23

Above: *Gawai Kenyalang*. This is one of the most important Iban ceremonies, involving the carving of an elaborate wooden hornbill. In earlier times the festival was held to impart courage to young warriors before going to war. Nowadays it is held to encourage *bejalai*, where young men leave the longhouse, travel and work for a few years, and return bearing riches and knowledge. Ngemah River, 1985.

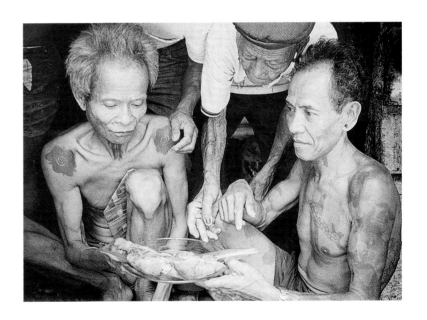

Right: *Gawai Kenyalang*. Iban Elders examining the liver of a freshly killed pig, to ensure the success of the *Gawai*. Augury is a very important part of the Iban religion, and any irregularity in the appearance of the internal organs is believed to be a message from the gods. Ngemah River, 1985.

Above: View from the longhouse door. The ladder is a single piece of *belian* (ironwood). Nanga Sumpa, Batang Ai, 1994.

Above: Ruai (interior verandah) of Nanga Sumpa longhouse. Batang Ai, 1994.

Above: Early morning at Nanga Sumpa longhouse. Batang Ai, 1994.

Above: Iban *Gawai Antu*, an extravagant and rarely-held feast in honour of the longhouse's ancestors. *Lemambang* (bards) recite from memory the entire history of the Iban people, and call upon the spirits to accept the offerings laid out for them. The bards may wear suits and ties instead of loin cloths nowadays, but the ritual is just as stirring, and the holy rice wine in the bowls they are carrying still represents the blood of their enemies. Betong, 1993.

Left: A proud mother looks on as her daughters prepare for the *Gawai Dayak* (harvest festival) celebration. Nanga Sumpa. Batang Ai, 1994.

Above: An Iban boat builder takes a well-earned break from constructing a wooden longboat. These tough little craft are constructed from three planks of wood, using nothing more sophisticated than an adze and a hand-saw. Ulu Tatau, 1962.

Opposite: Iban girls dressed in their traditional costumes. The rich brocade fabrics and silver ornaments are complemented by the *sugu tinggi*, an exquisite silver head-dress. Skrang River, 1979.

Left: Iban man with fighting cock. Birds such as these are highly prized by the Iban, and are carefully fed and nurtured before a competition. Lemanak River, 1999.

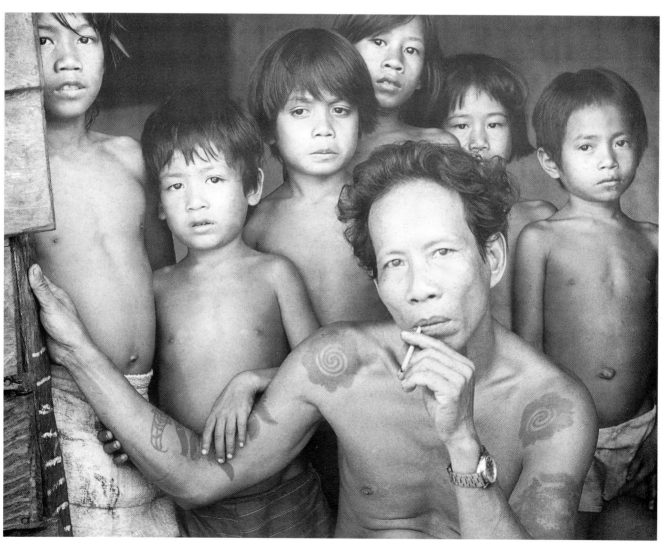

Above: Two generations of Iban. An atmospheric shot taken at the door of a remote longhouse. Ulu Tatau, 1985.

Below: The river is an essential part of Iban life, providing transport, drinking water and a place to wash and bathe. Here a young woman bathes in the river, carefully covering herself with her *sarong* to preserve her modesty. Kemena River, 1960.

SARAWAK
Kajang

The term "Kajang" is used to describe the various minor
ethnic groups that live in Central Sarawak, mainly on the
upper reaches of the Rejang River. These tribes - the
Kejaman, Punan Bah, Punan Kakus, Tanjong, Sekapan and
Lahanan - are distinct sub-groups of the Orang Ulu. Kajang
art, culture and social organisation is similar to their Kayan
and Kenyah neighbours. For many years they eked out a
precarious living in the buffer zone between the warring
Iban and Kayan.

Guardian figures outside a Punan Bah longhouse. Upper Rejang River, 1999.

A Punan Kakus elder proudly displays his ear-pendants, intricately carved from hornbill ivory. The objects in his upper ears are the fangs of a clouded leopard. Kakus River, Ulu Tatau, 1998.

An eldely Punan Bah lady with extensive tattoos on her hands and lower arms. General styles of wearing tattoos differ amongst the various Orang Ulu groups. Designs and the positioning of tattoos also vary from group to group. The Kajang tattoo their feet, hands and arms. Unlike the Kayan they do not tattoo their legs, except for small calf tattoos. Upper Rejang River, 1998.

A Kajang lady wearing brass earrings and dressed in her best attire for the the Belaga Regatta. Belaga, 1979.

Right: Two Kajang boys play around with their fathers' home-made bamboo pipes, whilst their friends gather around. Ulu Belaga, 1977.

Opposite: A Punan Kakus priestess and spirit medium, dressed for a healing ritual. As in most Orang Ulu communities, women are mainly responsible for religious activities. Kakus River, Ulu Tatau 1998.

Right: A Kajang *Salong*. This elegant wooden tomb atop a stout *belian* pole houses the remains of a Kajang aristocrat. Such tombs are still commonly used for high-ranking members of most Orang Ulu tribes. Kakus River, Ulu Tatau, 1973.

SARAWAK
Kayan

The Kayan are the largest of the Orang Ulu groups, living mainly in the Upper Rejang and Upper Baram river areas, with many more over the border in Central and Eastern Kalimantan. They are amongst Sarawak's most musical and artistic peoples, producing superb handicrafts and making fine musical instruments, most notable of which is the lute-like *sape*.

A Kayan woman sits at the door of her longhouse apartment at Uma Belor. This longhouse with the elaborate "tree of life" mural on the wall now lies abandoned, as Uma Belor was one of the many Orang Ulu longhouses affected by the Bakun dam project. In 1998 the whole community moved to a new longhouse at the Asap resettlement area. Balui River, 1995.

Lihan Hang, a Kayan *Penghulu* (chief), dressed up for a celebration. The warrior's skull cap, embroidered with beads and covered in tufts of goat hair, is often worn on formal occasions. *Penghulu* Lihan had travelled from Long Murum to Kapit to take part in a remembrance ceremony for the Great Peacemaking of 1921. This historic ceremony marked the end of inter-tribal warfare between the Iban and the Kayan. Kapit, 1994.

Above: Kesing Nyipa, a renowned Kayan *sape* player. In skilled hands, this lute-like instrument produces an exquisite, haunting melody. There is much friendly debate between the Kayan and the Kenyah over which tribe produces the best *sape* players. Ulu Belaga, 1977.

Opposite: A Kayan mother and her daughter try ice cream for the very first time. They had come from Ulu Tubau to Bintulu to attend the Regatta celebrations. This is one of Dennis' earliest photos, taken when he was a student. Bintulu, 1952.

Above: The intense concentration on the face of this elderly Kayan lady reflects the skill she brings to her art. Many upper-class women are not required to do farm work, and can therefore dedicate much of their time to becoming superb craftswomen. This lady is splitting rattan to make a headband similar to the one she is wearing. Long Miri, Baram River, 1996.

Opposite: The scorched remains of a tree trunk tower above a Kayan farmer as he takes a break from preparing the land for planting hill padi. Apoh River, Ulu Baram, 1990.

42

SARAWAK
Kelabit

The Kelabit are one of the smallest of Sarawak's ethnic groups, numbering less than 5,000. A sub-group of the Orang Ulu, most Kelabit live in large longhouses scattered around the Bario Highlands - a remote plateau without road or river transport - or in the upper reaches of the Baram river. They are closely related to the Lun Bawang in Sarawak, and the Lun Dayeh of Southern Sabah and Kalimantan. The fragrant Bario rice grown on their terraced padi fields is in great demand throughout Sarawak. Despite their isolation, the Kelabit are remarkably well educated and successful in business, politics and the professions, a fact they attribute to their devout Christian faith.

Above: This Kelabit lady has brought her young grandson along to the longhouse tap. It is very common for Kelabit women to wear fine antique bead necklaces even when performing the household chores. Bario, 1973.

Left: Kelabit woman packing cooked rice in leaves. In the cool Bario Highlands, longhouse life revolves around the family hearth rather than the longhouse verandah. Bario, 1973.

Opposite: Two Kelabit girls, wearing their finest beads and earrings to welcome visitors. Bario, 1973.

Opposite: Kelabit Mother and child. The clusters of brass earrings and the beadwork skullcap are still everyday wear for many Kelabit women. Bario, 1973.

Below: Two Kelabit elders wearing hornbill ivory ear pendants. Hornbill ivory is a very difficult material to work with and very few people gain sufficient skill to carve intricate designs. Traditionally, only those who were able to carve hornbill ivory would wear such earrings. Bario, 1973.

Kenyah

The Kenyah are the second largest Orang Ulu group, sharing the upper reaches of the Rejang and Baram rivers with the Kayan. Kenyah culture and social organisation is very similar to that of the Kayan, but their language is quite different. They construct massive longhouses, some holding more than a hundred families, which are decorated with colourful, intricate "tree of life" murals. Like the Kayan, they are excellent artists and musicians, and there is always a good-humoured argument between the two tribes as to who produces the finest *sape* players.

Opposite: Portrait of a Kenyah lady. Her elongated ears, a sign of great beauty amongst all Orang Ulu peoples, have been stretched with brass ear pendants since she was a small girl. Long Jeeh, Ulu Baram, 1995.

Above: A woman performs the hornbill feather dance. This is regarded as the most difficult of all the Kenyah women's dances, requiring great skill and concentration to effectively mimic the movements of the rhinoceros hornbill. Tinjar River, 1972.

Above: A Kenyah woman smoking a home-made cigarette. Both the Kenyah and the Kayan cultivate fiercely strong dark shag tobacco, which they roll into conical cigarettes using dried banana or palm leaves. Lio Matoh, Ulu Baram, 1995.

Opposite: Young women with children. Kenyah girls are expected to help look after their younger siblings and relatives, early training for motherhood. This photograph was taken on Dennis's first visit to the Tinjar River, and the quietly dignified beauty of his subjects helps to explain why he returned there many times. Tinjar River, 1970.

Longhouse hospitality. This stunningly-clad Kenyah lady is welcoming guests to her longhouse with a glass of *borak*, a potent rice wine (despite what is written on the bottle). Kenyah women take great pride in their brewing skills, and welcoming a visitor with a shop-bought beverage would be a severe breach of etiquette. Long San, Ulu Baram , 1995.

Above: Kenyah women singing a praise-song to welcome guests into the longhouse. Kenyah praise-songs, which describe the achievement and attributes of the visitor, are reserved for distinguished guests, and are usually composed on the spot by the singer. Long Palai, Ulu Baram, 1995.

Right: These two young Kenyah girls are wearing traditional embroidered dresses and beadwork. Kenyah traditions are still strong, but the practice of elongating earlobes is dying out, as this picture demonstrates. In fact, many young Kenyah women own a pair of clip-on false earlobes to be worn when performing traditional dances. Long San, Ulu Baram, 1995.

Opposite: A Kenyah mother and her children. Tinjar River, 1972.

Below: Wedding guests. These Kenyah women have placed their sun-hats on the floor and donned their festive caps for the occasion. Long San, Ulu Baram, 1973.

Above: A Kenyah naming ceremony. When children are born they are only given temporary names, for their character and personality must first develop before their parents can choose a suitable name. They must then be named in front of the whole longhouse, so every 3 or 4 years a grand naming ceremony is held for all the un-named children. These two boys are wearing name tags with their new names. The baby carriers, in which they were carried as infants, will then be ceremonially abandoned and kept as heirlooms. Long Selatong, Ulu Baram, 1993.

Opposite: Kenyah mother and child. The beautifully decorated baby carrier is both practical and elegant, and allows the mother to take her baby with her wherever she goes. Ulu Baram, 1978.

SARAWAK
Malay

The Malays are the dominant ethnic group throughout most of Maritime Southeast Asia. In Sarawak they comprise about 22% of the population. Execlusively Muslim, Sarawak's Malays trace their ancestry from all over the region; some are descended from Brunei Malays, others from migrants from Java, Sumatra, Sulawasi and Mindanao, and some from indigenous people who embraced Islam many generations ago. The Malays are predominantly coastal people, fishing and growing wet padi, but in Sarawak they also form a substantial urban business and professional class, and Malay *kampungs* (villages) can be found in or near almost every town in the state.

Malay woman pounding dried shrimps to make *belacan*. This fermented shrimp paste is an essential ingredient in most Malay cooking, and the finest *belacan* is produced by cottage industries like this. Kampung Buntal, 1988.

Above: Kampung Buntal, an idyllic Malay fishing village famous for its seafood restaurants. Kampung Buntal, 1988.

Below: Two Malay children watch the photographer from the window of their *atap* house. Kampung Buntal, 1990.

Opposite: A group of Malay schoolboys taking part in a parade to commemorate the birth of the Prophet Muhammad. They are chanting holy verses to the rhythm of the drums as they march through town. Miri, 1967.

Left: An elderly Malay fisherman rests on the verandah of his *atap* house, which is constructed entirely from nipah palm and split bamboo. Kampung Buntal, 1988.

Below: A sensitive portrait of a Malay fisherman. Kampung Buntal, 1989.

An elderly Malay man waits patiently at the jetty for the fishing boats to return, so that he can take his pick from the fresh catch. Bintulu, 1960.

61

SARAWAK
Melanau

The Melanau, numbering approximately 6% of the population, live mainly along the coastal strip of Sarawak between Kuala Rejang in the south and Bintulu in the north. Their economy is based on the growing and processing of sago, and they are also expert fishermen and boat builders. They are perfect examples of Sarawak's famous religious tolerance, with Muslims, Christians and Pagans living happily side-by-side.

Typical Melanau village at Kampung Tellian near Mukah. The Melanau, traditionally fishermen and sago growers, built their houses on or near rivers to allow easy access to the sea and effortless transport of sago logs. Mukah, 1993.

Above: Kaul Festival. Kaul is the annual festival for the god of the sea, celebrated every year at Mukah. Here, *seraheng*, brightly decorated ceremonial baskets containing offerings, are prepared and preliminary blessings recited. Mukah, 1994.

Above: Kaul Festival - The Presentation. Once the preliminary rituals are finished, the offerings are transferred into beautifully decorated boats, which are then placed on the shore at the mouth of the river, as gifts for the sea spirits. Mukah, 1994.

Above: Sago logs tied up to await processing at Kampung Tellian. Mukah, 1993

Opposite: Kaul Festival -The *Tibou*. The *tibou* is where young Melanau men prove their manhood by taking part in a boisterous and sometimes dangerous game on a giant swing. One man starts the rope swinging and others jump on board from the adjacent stand, swinging higher and higher until eventually someone loses his grip and the whole group has a bruising collision with the hard ground. Mukah, 1994.

Above: Sago processing. This lady is preparing sago starch the traditional way, treading the sago palm shavings into a pulp which she then washes out with water. The liquefied starch is gathered in the tray below, and is dried in the sun before cooking. Matu, 1993.

Opposite: Portrait of a Melanau fisherman. This old man has spent all his life fishing in a small open boat on the South China Sea. His proud, weather-beaten face tells its own story. Mukah, 1994.

SARAWAK
Penan

The Penan are traditionally nomadic hunter-gatherers, inhabiting the deep jungles of central and northern Sarawak. Today, many have become settled agriculturalists, living in longhouse-type communities. However, even the settled Penan return frequently to the forest to hunt and to gather jungle produce. Despite their nomadic lifestyle, they are excellent craftsmen; the men are expert blacksmiths and blowpipe makers, whilst the women produce exquisite baskets and rattan mats, regarded as the finest in Borneo.

Opposite: Portrait of a Penan elder in a typically thoughtful pose. Long Akah, Ulu Baram, 1972.

Below: A Penan family on the move. When they shift to a new location, all their worldly possessions must be carried in huge rattan backpacks. Most Penan can trek all day through some of the roughest terrain in Borneo with a full load on their backs. Sela'an River, Ulu Baram, 1978.

Above: Daybreak outside the Penan hut or *lamin tana'* (temporary shelter). The Penan build these shelters in a matter of hours, abandoning them when the local supply of game and wild sago is exhausted. A group of hunters have returned and the children proudly display their fathers' catch of squirrels. Near Long San, Ulu Baram, 1968.

Opposite: The Penan generally have a shorter life span than other ethnic groups in Sarawak owing to their tough jungle lifestyle. Seeing a Penan as old as this wizened elder is very rare. Yet despite his great age he could still move about the jungle with the aid of his walking stick. Long Akah, Ulu Baram, 1978.

Above: A group of Penan children. Although clothing is hardly necessary at this age, they wear many charms and amulets to ward off evil spirits. Silat River, Ulu Baram, 1970.

Opposite: A Penan elder prepares for the hunt. His blowpipe, the result of weeks of painstaking work, is a deadly accurate hunting weapon for all kinds of game. Although many Penan possess shotguns, the blowpipe is still widely used, particularly for smaller animals. Sela'an River, Ulu Baram, 1978.

Left: Although they are frequently on the move, the Penan are as fond of pets as any other people. Layun, Ulu Baram, 1987.

Below: After the hunt, it's time to relax. This young Penan man is playing a *kelure*, a traditional wind instrument fashioned from gourds and bamboo. Layun, Ulu Baram, 1987.

SARAWAK
Sebop

The Sebop, one of the smaller *Orang Ulu* groups, are closely related to the Kenyah and live on the Tinjar River. The Sebop of Long Luyang (where these photos were taken) moved from the Menavan River in Usun Apau to the headwaters of the Tinjar River in the late 19th century. When these photos were taken in the early 1970's, Long Luyang was a 45 door longhouse and home to over 400 people.

Opposite: Sebop Mother and child. Like most *Orang Ulu* groups, Sebop women traditionally wear brass pendants in their elongated ears. Long Luyang, Tinjar River, 1974.

Left: A typical *Orang Ulu* haircut takes shape. This traditional style consists of a shaved back and sides, a straight, cropped fringe at the front and a long pony-tail. Long Luyang, Tinjar River, 1970.

SABAH
Bajau

The predominately Muslim Bajau make up around 10% of Sabah's population. They arrived in Sabah from the southern Philippines around 200 years ago. They were often called sea-gypsies as they traditionally lived on their boats and roamed the seas in search of fish and other sea products. Although some still live this nomadic lifestyle, most have settled, either inland or in coastal fishing villages. The Land Bajau are farmers and cattle rearers and are centred around Kota Belud and Tuaran. The Bajau Laut (Sea Bajau) live in and around the waters and islands near the port of Semporna in Eastern Sabah.

Left: Two Bajau girls fan themselves whilst waiting for the bride and groom to arrive at a Bajau wedding ceremony. Kota Belud, 1980.

Opposite: A Bajau horseman, one of the aptly-named "Cowboys of Borneo," dressed up for the weekly *tamu,* or market. Kota Belud, 1980.

Above: Two brightly coloured Bajau Laut *prahu* make for the fishing grounds. Semporna, 1987.

Left: The traditional Bajau Laut's entire life is lived at sea, so even the cooking is done on board these small boats. Semporna, 1987.

Below: The cramped living quarters of a Bajau Laut houseboat make for very close-knit families. Semporna, 1987.

A Bajau Laut fisherman prepares to set sail. Semporna, 1987.

Above: A Bajau man awaits a buyer for his buffalo at the weekly *tamu*, or market. Kota Belud, 1980.

Opposite: Portrait of an elderly Bajau man. Tuaran, 1968.

SABAH
Kadazan/Dusun

The Kadazan/Dusun are the largest ethnic group in Sabah, living mostly on the west coast and in the interior areas of the state. They are traditionally agriculturalists although nowadays Kadazan/Dusun are found in all sectors of the economy. Although the majority of Kadazan/Dusun are Christian many of their cultural activities still retain elements of their animist past. For example, during the harvest festival or *pesta kaamatan*, priestesses or *bobohizans* perform various rituals to appease the rice spirit.

Above: The rice harvest dance is an essential part of *Pesta Kaamatam*, the Kadazan/Dusun harvest festival held at the end of May. Keningau, 1987.

Opposite: A young Kadazan/Dusun girl sits astride her father's buffalo. In the background is Mount Kinabalu, the highest mountain in Southeast Asia. The Kadazan/Dusun are expert rice farmers, extracting two crops a year from their irrigated padi fields. This back-breaking work is made easier with the assistance of buffaloes. Tampassuk, near Kota Belud, 1968.

Above: A Kadazan/Dusun lady at the market. All her wares are carried in her enormous basketware backpack. Tambunan, 1985.

Right: A family set off for the fields near Kundasan, in the foothills of Mount Kinabalu. Kundasan's temperate climate and high rainfall make it an ideal area for farming and market gardening, but the rugged terrain and strong winds ensure that life is not easy. Kundasan, 1985.

Above: An elderly lady covering her face with her hat. Like most Borneo peoples, the Kadazan/Dusun are expert basket weavers. Tambunan, 1985.

Left: A group of boys hitch a ride from a friendly water buffalo. Kota Belud, 1980.

Above: A woman carries her basket full of pineapples to market in Kundasan. Mount Kinabalu is in the background. The Kundasan fruit and vegetable market is famous for its fresh produce, and the pineapples have to be tasted to be believed. Kundasan, 1980.

Opposite: Two Kadazan/Dusun girls in traditional dress. Kota Belud, 1968.

SABAH
Murut

The Murut inhabit the hilly regions of Southwest Sabah, close to the borders with Sarawak and Kalimantan. Formerly the most warlike of Sabah's ethnic groups, their traditional economy is based around hill rice and cassava. The Murut have largely abandoned their previous longhouse life to settle in large villages made up of individual wooden or brick houses.

A girl makes some final adjustments to her friend's head-dress before a Murut cultural troupe performs at the harvest festival celebrations. Keningau, 1987.

A Murut lady takes a drink of *tapai*, a traditional rice wine, using bamboo straws. The straws have a special significance - when strangers came to the longhouse in earlier times they could sip from the communal jug with their own drinking straw, thus ensuring it was not poisoned. The jugs they are drinking from are centuries-old family heirlooms - most Borneo people believe it is impossible to brew good rice wine in a modern plastic or metal container. Sapulut, 1985.

A Murut family group on the verandah of their longhouse. Note the absence of the young men, who have moved away to seek employment in the towns and cities, returning only during holidays and harvest time. Keningau, 1987.

Right: Murut villagers return to their homes over a long and flimsy-looking suspension bridge. Retaining one's dignity whilst crossing these bridges requires some practice, as they tend to sway wildly in rhythm with your steps. Sapulut, 1985.

Below: Navigating the rapids. The rivers of the Murut heartland are difficult to navigate except in the rainy season. The easiest way to get this small boat through the rapids is by punting with long poles. A larger and heavier craft requires the passengers to get their feet wet. Pensiangan, 1985.

SABAH
Rungus

The Rungus are mainly found in the Kudat district in northern Sabah. They are a sub-group of the Kadazan/Dusun and have their own distinctive language, customs, dress and oral literature. The Rungus traditionally lived in longhouses made up of individual family apartments. These impressive dwellings were previously built from wood, bamboo and atap, although today it is rare to see thatched-roof Rungus longhouses as corrugated zinc is now the favoured roofing material. The Rungus have a rich and colourful culture and have managed to retain many of their traditions and beliefs.

Above: An elderly Rungus lady at work on a back strap loom. The Rungus are renowned weavers, producing finely woven textiles which incorporate intricate traditional motifs. Kudat, 1985.

Opposite: Traditionally all Rungus women wore heavy brass coils around their arms, legs and necks. Brass arm coils are often accompanied by a white shell bracelets. Rings of brass may also be worn around the waist. Although it is still quite common to see older women wearing brass coils, especially around their arms, this custom is dying out amongst the younger generation. Kudat, 1980.

Opposite: A young mother and her child sit in the *apad*, the common gallery of the longhouse. The Rungus longhouse is divided into two distinct areas - the *apad* or common gallery and the *ongkob* or enclosed compartment area. The *ongkob* is made up of a kitchen and eating area called the *langsang* and a raised platform where women and children sleep called the *tingkang*. Older boys and male visitors sleep in the *apad*. Kudat, 1985.

Right: A lady winnowing maize on the *apad* of a Rungus longhouse. Kudat, 1985.

Above: A group of children look out of an opening in the thatched *atap* roof of the longhouse. Rungus longhouses were traditionally made from wood, bamboo and *atap*. However today, corrugated iron is often the preferred roofing material, replacing the thatched *atap*. Although there are still a number of traditional longhouses in Kudat, many Rungus families are opting to build their own individual houses. Kudat, 1985.

Opposite: Rungus elders take time out at Kudat market. Although western style clothing is now common, Rungus men often dress up in their traditional finery, particularly when they venture out from the longhouse. They normally wear baggy trousers and a short tunic accompanied by a coloured waist sash and a *sigal*, the traditional embroidered headgear. Kudat, 1980.

Above: A Rungus lady adjusts her headpiece before setting out for market. Kudat, 1980.